Get Out of Control:

Finding Freedom in Letting Go!

Acknowledgments

During any season of challenge or hardship, it is essential to keep one's priorities in focus. Faith, family, and friends are central in keeping grounded when the plagues of a broken world assault peace. As we finish this manuscript together, we are hunkered down in our home at the peak of the Covid-19 virus outbreak. In the Psalms, there is a beautiful word "Selah" that has great significance in times like this. Selah instructs the reader to pause and reflect upon the truths declared in the Psalm. It would appear we are in a Selah season where the entire planet has been forced to slow down, pause, and to call upon God for His divine intervention. It is also a time to reflect on the current circumstances of our lives. This is when our faith, family, and friends come into a greater focus for the essentials of love, hope, and significance. To love God and to love one another are the two greatest commands. We trust that this book will further grow these essentials in your life. We encourage you to read with a heart influenced by Selah.

In alignment to these ideals, we want to give special acknowledgment and appreciation to the many amazing friends and family members who have contributed to this work. There has been a lot of counsel, edits, suggestions, and advice that came from the people we dearly love and respect. First and foremost, our family has helped live out the principles in this book as we have continued to guide and influence one another in our mutual growth. Thank you, Madi, Julia, Shiloh, Michael, Preston, Matt, Chelsea, Kennedy, Brody, Peyton, Bryson, and Catherine for your loving and joyful witness and input. Also, with great gratitude, we have benefitted immensely from the insights and suggestions of Denise and Josh Jones, Alexa, and Josh Randall, Krista and Chris Francis, Jeanette Bradley, Chris Mefford, and our many Rock Church friends. And as iron sharpens iron, it has been a joy to develop these thoughts and insights together as a husband and wife. We have been challenged to be more vulnerable, gracious, and understanding of our different points of view. Truly, God is faithful! He is continuing to teach us to get out of control. It's one thing to write about the things we need to do to become more authentic and virtuous, and quite another to actually live this out on a daily basis. To all of our friends, family, and ministry partners, we say a big, "thank you!" We love and appreciate you for your investment in our life. We are blessed in God's favor.

Forward

Is there any greater lie than the one we continually tell ourselves – that we are somehow "in control" of our lives? I contend – and history has proven - that the answer is "no." And yet, in spite of all the evidence to the contrary, we continue to try. The desire to control is neither new nor unique to our generation. From the beginning of time, humans have tried to play God - not only in our own lives but also in the lives of others. This desire stems from a number of factors, including an oversized ego, an undersized faith, fear, love, doubt, a sense of over-responsibility, or just wanting things to turn out our way.

Most of the time, there's nothing inherently wrong with our desire to control. It's completely normal to want to control the things we can - like our schedules, how we raise our children, where we live, what we do for work, who we marry, and who we call our "friends." But our controlling natures get us into trouble when we let them interfere with God's plan for our lives and others', causing division, chaos, frustration, and broken relationships. Fortunately, no matter how hard we try to take over, God is always, ultimately in control. It may not seem like He is, especially when things aren't going our way. But that's when we have to remind ourselves that our view of what's good for us is totally different from God's, because our perspective is limited, while His is eternal. God is the author of the beginning, middle, and end of every situation, and promises to work all things out "for the good of those who love Him" (Romans 8:28). It's up to us to take Him at His word, rest in the knowledge that He has a perfect plan for our lives, and believe that He will bring it to pass.

I've walked with God for over 25 years now; long enough to know and experience His goodness. If you'd asked me, I'd have told you - without hesitation - that I believed He was in control of my life, and of everything that happens in this world. Before reading this book, I thought I was rock solid in that conviction. But after reading this book, I'm aware of the circumstances and relationships I subconsciously wrote off as "impossible" for God to change. Believing that lie caused me to think that I was on my own, which made me controlling and manipulative in ways I never intended to be.

That's why I'm so grateful to Karen and Mickey – two of the wisest people I know – for sharing their own struggles with control, and how they are learning to get out of control. Their advice has helped me defeat the enemy's lies, and reign in my controlling nature, which was destroying my marriage, my work relationships, my friendships, and my faith. The battle is ongoing, but the tide has turned, thanks to the truths they've shared in this book.

So, whether you're a full-on control freak like me or someone who just dabbles in control from time to time, I pray that this book gives you the spiritual revelation, wisdom, and encouragement you need to break free from the lie that you are, or could ever be, in control of your life. Remember:

GOD IS IN CONTROL!

Denise Gitsham-Jones

Table of Contents

Preface

Preface

You're not going to want to read this book because it's going to hurt so good. It's a tough sell encouraging people to let go of their pride and ego. Yet, discovering liberty from self-dominance provides a pathway of peace that truly surpasses all understanding.

As you read, we hope you'll find this freedom and discover a way of living that will transform your relationships. It is paradoxical that Jesus declared that in order to be rich, we must become poor, to be a leader we must follow, and to be great we must become servants. In the same vein, in order to be free, we must give up our preeminence, as well as our desire to have our own way.

A number of years ago, I (Karen) was given a memorable experience from the Lord. We were visiting our oldest daughter, son-in-law, and grandkids in Italy. They had moved to Tuscany for a year of adventure, and Mickey and I were able to join in the fun for a few weeks. On the third day, we were still adjusting to the new time zone and my sleep schedule was completely off. I was in desperate need of a good night's sleep.

It was in this context that I fell asleep exhausted from the day and slept through the night thinking it had only been a few moments. However, when I awoke, I longed desperately to return to my dream world. I had experienced the most amazing dream that anyone could hope to have in their lifetime. I had been soaring with

God through the vast Milky Way Galaxy, past the stars, diving into the auroras of the outermost limits of the heavens. The drop in my stomach as we journeyed was the feeling you get on a wild roller coaster ride. As you might imagine, my fists were white-knuckled, with the tightest grip on God's wrists as He held mine. The laughter, joy, and wonder I experienced was beyond words. God spoke to me at one point and said, "Let go." He wanted me to let go of His wrists! "I have you," He said. But did I trust Him? Could I let go with complete confidence? Yes, I could! From the depths of my heart, I knew I could trust Him because of the years He had so faithfully revealed Himself to me in the Scriptures and in life's painful seasons.

In this remarkable dream, I had a deep faith in my Savior and I knew that He had me in His mighty hands. I had nothing to worry about. I could be free and let Him take me where He wished. So, I let go and was under His complete control. I felt freedom and joy that were beyond words. I was in ecstasy. Then I suddenly awoke, to the unfamiliar walls that surrounded my bed, and the strong aroma of Italian coffee brewing. I had slept through the night! It was such a vivid experience and seemed to be way beyond a regular dream. I can still recall the exhilaration of soaring through the galaxies and seeing the vastness in my mind's eye. So, I laid there still. I closed my eyes again, longing to go back into that time with Jesus. There was so much love and connection with the Father. It was so rich in His presence.

I have come to realize that this level of intimacy with the Father is what God desires for each of us. In the awesome heart of God, it is His incredible pleasure to declare those who believe in Him, that we are His beloved children. It is therefore essential that we know and believe what God says about our true identity in Him so that we can experience this freedom. We are all unique individuals; utterly one of a kind. We are valued and loved by God and He wants to be intimate with each of us. The world's values are not the measure we should use to evaluate our worth and dignity. We are only defined by what God says.

The truest way to know who you are and why you are on this earth stems from understanding what the Bible declares about you. Culture, media, parents, siblings, coworkers, feelings, traumas, and accomplishments in all of their intertwining complexities do not define us or give us value. These different experiences in life go deep into the soul and may even seem to scream at us, but they are only opinions at best. One of our favorite Bible teachers, John Piper, shares his conclusion about our primary purpose in life this way, "The chief end of humanity is to glorify God by enjoying Him forever." By basking in the Lord's presence, whatever our circumstances may be, our ultimate purpose is fulfilled.

Above all things, we want to encourage you to take time to search out the depths of God's heart and who He declares you are in Him. Sit, be still, and meditate on His Word. Doing so will help you soar to new heights with your Creator. Let every lie of the world be muted in His company. Enjoy Him! This will bring you endless amounts of wonder, love, joy, and freedom in His presence! As Scripture says, "In Your presence is fullness of joy, at Your right hand are pleasures forevermore."[1]

Sadly, many have a wrong perspective of who God is. In people's pain, they often conclude that God is nowhere. They feel that God has forsaken them or that He doesn't even exist. After all, they ask, why didn't He deliver them from heartache and pain? In God's design, He gave humanity freedom of choice, which accounts for much of the evil in the world. But in the midst of our suffering, the Bible also reveals that God brings redemption, healing, and significance to our pain and brokenness. Our God is that One who promises to never leave us or forsake us. It is pretty crazy, but deep down inside many people are of the mindset that they are actually able to control God. This is the ultimate deception in the war on control. In the midst of life's challenges, individuals determine their own opinions about who God is and define God according to their own liking. In a sense, these people make God in their image, when in reality it is God who made us in His. Ask God to reveal more of Himself to you. Give him permission to release you from any wrong beliefs that keep you from letting go. And prepare to experience the fullness of knowing that you are fully loved and cared for

---

[1] Psalm 16:11 (NKJV)

by the Father who loves you more than anyone ever could.

Chapter One
An Invitation to Freedom

No matter what role you play in life — as a parent, sibling, friend, teenager, roommate, employee, boss, husband, or wife—you likely deal with something common to the rest of humanity; the overwhelming struggle to CONTROL. Being "in control" of your life can feel comforting and safe, but, like a chameleon, control disguises itself in a variety of ways to hide its complex motives. Most of us don't even recognize its presence in our lives. Control is an expert at camouflaging itself with excuses, justifications, and blame-shifting. Our hope is that you will discover where control has been lurking in the shadows of your own heart, and be set free from its grip.

We invite you to join us in this discovery of the steps that can be taken to free yourself from the illusion and desire to control your own life, and that of others. This is not to say that we have mastered this challenge ourselves. Through over forty years of marriage, four adult kids and four grandchildren, we are still learning to let go. We have been involved with countless individuals and their troubled relationships, marriages, and/or family trauma. Helping people work through relational conflict has been a huge part of our lives. Our many roles and experiences as counselor, professor, pastor, chaplain, and friend have afforded us a vast education in the study of human brokenness. We have worked with men and women in a variety of settings; one-on-one appointments, small groups, university classrooms, and large conferences, and we've observed that age isn't a factor in this struggle. We've also noticed that this dynamic is not limited only to those strong-willed people who overtly attempt to control and dominate others. Control is a toxic struggle that infects every human being at various stress points in our lives, and it is very effective at disrupting our families, friendships, and work relationships.

Control takes on a variety of forms and manifests itself differently for everyone. The reasons we feel the need to control others and/or circumstances vary widely. They may stem from fear, learned behavior from guardians, neglect, insecurity, or past trauma. Think back for a moment and see if you can recall yourself saying something along the lines of, "I am just trying to help" or, "You shouldn't do it that way." These are common phrases we all use to manipulate or influence others, even if they're true! The two of us look back now and recognize how these seemingly innocent exchanges were actually camouflaged attempts to control. It may have been something as simple as backseat driving or outright manipulation of someone to agree with our own ways. These controlling motives are scattered along the paths of many of our relationships.

Serving in academics and ministry for over four decades has afforded us the privilege of serving a wide variety of people. We have heard countless wonderful stories of people's lives as they encounter the ups and downs of our broken world. One such miracle was our ministry friend, Kevin, when he learned a lesson of surrender in a mysterious way. While pounding fence posts with a heavy-duty hydraulic post-pounder on his ranch a large chunk of a wooden post shot out and crushed his skull. He was rushed to the hospital in semi-consciousness and wasn't expected to live. Given the minuscule odds of surviving the surgery, his family was called in to say goodbye before he underwent the operation. Fervent prayers went up before the Lord and God graciously brought Kevin through the surgery. With a titanium plate now in his skull he regained consciousness and endured a prolonged season of rehabilitation.

Months later, he was scheduled to have an early morning MRI to assess his progress. While lying in the MRI tube, right before the radiologist flipped the switch on, a supervising nurse halted the MRI. He was told to exit the tube and that he would need to reschedule as they had overbooked too many appointments that day. And understandably annoyed, Kevin was forced to exit the room, irritated that he'd been displaced to accommodate a grouchy nurse's scheduling preferences.

In the days that followed, Kevin played with his daughters in his kitchen and while at play they put one of the refrigerator magnets on his forehead, which surprisingly stuck. Giggling together, they placed several more magnets on his head and they all held fast. A bit puzzled, Kevin, retrieved a letter given to him by the surgeon explaining that the implant in his head was

100% titanium, non-magnetic and MRI compatible. Confused as to why the magnets were sticking to his head, he scheduled an appointment with his neurosurgeon to discuss his concern. During the exam, Kevin displayed to his doctor the discovery that his titanium plate held the magnets. The surgeon was immediately alarmed and, in a panic, he did some testing and soon discovered that the plate in Kevin's forehead was faulty. Arrangements were immediately made to have the plate replaced. The doctor also told Kevin that if the technician had flipped the MRI switch on, it would have killed him instantly. The grumpy supervising nurse that he'd been so annoyed with turned out to have saved his life. What an amazing display of God's gracious providence, revealing His loving protection and providence through inconvenience and frustration!

How is it that we so often let the circumstantial challenges and interruptions to our plans and control, disrupt our sense of peace and harmony? How can we learn to live a life that is humbly surrendered to God's providence without becoming a cynical passive fatalist? And how can we learn to let go of moments of exasperation to experience peace in the midst of a storm?

Let's start by defining control. Control means "to exercise an authoritative or dominating influence over; to hold in restraint, to regulate, to influence; to master, dominate or restrain." Yikes!

In his book Control Freak, Dr. Les Parrott III, who confesses to being a recovering control maniac, says that "the soul of control is fueled by anxiety and nurtured by feelings of extreme vulnerability and a fragile self-confidence."[2] In other words, the root of control lies in our feelings of insecurity, fears, and helplessness; things that none of us want controlling us!

Wouldn't it be great to learn how to develop a soul of peace that is fueled by faith and love, and allows for healthy and authentic vulnerability in our closest relationships? In this book, we will learn to take on the mind of Christ and to experience the freedom available to us through God's transforming grace. As you read along with us, the following questions may surge from your heart: What do I do now? Will I be able to even recognize this in my thoughts and actions? How do I deal with this relentless propensity to do things my own way? What can I do to guard against being a controlling person? How do I best deal with the other controlling people in my life? What is the antidote for this struggle? If so, be encouraged that the very purpose of this study is to discover answers to these specific questions.

Part of our challenge is becoming self-aware of the areas of our lives in which we struggle with control. Most often honest feedback from others is the path to enlightenment. We embolden others to offer their feedback, by living out a moment-by-moment decision to remain humble and teachable in our relationships and

---

[2] Parrott III, Les. (2000). *The Control Freak: Coping with Those Around You. Taming the One Within.* Carol Stream, Illinois: Tyndale House Publishers.

conversations with them. We will be digging deep into our hearts to better discern our motives and the possible roots that trigger our behaviors. In the following chapters, we will explore the basis of these dynamics and help you understand how to move from veiled bondage to vulnerable freedom.

Reflect-Respond-Renew

Throughout this book, you will be asked to pause, reflect, and consider how certain aspects of control may be lurking beneath the surface of your actions. Below are some words we would like you to read. As you do, consider the painful periods in your life and relationships where your heart has been wounded. Let the Holy Spirit speak truth to your spirit as you ponder these areas.

What words stand out from the list below? What words stir up emotions? Can you identify why and when you felt this way?

Failure
Embarrassment
Abuse
Humiliation
Rejection
Abandonment
Addiction
Outbursts of anger/rage
Isolation
Insecurity
Indiscriminate fear
Overwhelmed/stressed
Financial loss
Divorce
The death of a loved one
A dominant parent

A traumatic incident

Pause for a moment and write down any feelings that arise in association with some of these words. As you read this book, become familiar with some of these potential prompts. This may help you identify where, when, and why control creeps into your thoughts and actions. Research shows that survival and self-preservation complicate our issues of personal identity, individual value, depression, and anxiety. Past trauma, big or small, is frequently discovered to be at the source of our current challenges, where we grow the need to feel in control of our subsequent perceived threats. Let's learn together how to get out of control and how to find freedom in letting go and trusting God!

Chapter Two
First Things First

Throughout this book, you will be challenged to make a significant change in your worldview. Most of us perceive life and circumstances from a "me-centered" position. What we think or believe determines how we view our reality and what we believe to be "true." However, in the beginning, God spoke the world into existence for His glorious purposes. This is His world and He has a plan and design for all things. We need to adjust our thinking to be in line with Biblical theology and its guidance for our relationships. This will even affect our view of our personal identity. But in order to get there, we must begin with a God-first and God-centered lens, rather than a me-centered one.

It may be helpful at this point to start at the very beginning: "In the beginning God."[3] It is here that we are given a glimpse into when and where our desire to control first took root. When God created man and woman, His intent was for a relationship that would bring Him glory and pleasure. God wanted to enjoy a love relationship with His children. Everything operated in complete harmony until Satan showed up and tempted Adam and Eve.

> "Now the serpent was more cunning than
> any beast of the field which the LORD
> God had made. And He said to the

---

[3] Genesis 1:1 (NKJV)

woman, 'Has God indeed said, 'You shall
not eat of every tree of the garden?' And
the woman said to the serpent, 'We may
eat the fruit of the trees of the garden; but
of the fruit of the tree which is in the
midst of the garden, God has said, 'You
shall not eat it, nor shall you touch it, lest
you die.' Then the serpent said to the
woman, 'You will not surely die. For God
knows that in the day you eat of it your
eyes will be opened, and you will be like
God, knowing good and evil.'"[4]

This is the moment when all the trouble began. At the
core, Adam and Eve wanted to be like God in
determining their own truth—to know good and evil.
But in Genesis 1:26-27, we are told that they were
already made in the image of God:

"Then God said, 'Let Us make man in
Our image, according to Our likeness; let
them have dominion over the fish of the
sea, over the birds of the air, and over the
cattle, over all the earth and over every
creeping thing that creeps on the earth.'
So God created man in His own image;
in the image of God He created him;
male and female He created them"
(NKJV).

---

[4] Genesis 3:1-4 (NKJV)

So ultimately, Adam and Eve were tempted to be God, rather than to reflect His image. It was this very same desire that fueled Satan's own fall from grace (see Isaiah 14:12-14). And throughout the Bible, there are countless tragic stories of people following his lead, by trying to control their own destinies, rather than surrendering to God's ways (see Judges 21:25, Jeremiah 7:24).

Back to Adam and Eve, however, what's interesting about their situation is that God gave them only one boundary. The Father loved them and gave them everything to enjoy in the garden of Eden – everything was called "good." There was only one thing He labeled as off-limits. But they were not content with the perfection of paradise, so they did what they wanted and stepped over the boundary that God had set for them.

Then came the bad part, the consequences of their selfish choice: "To the woman, He (God) said: 'I will greatly multiply your sorrow and your conception; in pain, you shall bring forth children; Your desire shall be for your husband, and he shall rule over you.'"[5] This curse was declared as a result of their disobedience and defiance of God. The Hebrew root of the word "desire" literally means to "overflow." So what God cursed Eve with is the desire to flood her husband with overflow – in other words, the desire to be in control! And as a result of the fall, the husband shall "rule over you," literally

---

5 Genesis 3:16 (NKJV)

meaning to "dominate," which again multiplies the potential conflict for control.

What may not be apparent to some of us is that ruling over another person is a destructive trait. Controlling others takes us out of God's intended design for relationships. God designed us for companionship, not for dominance and inequality. Adam and Eve were equal to one another, and God walked with them in harmony, love, and peace. But when the curse of sin entered the world, control, division, discord, and disagreements were activated, not just between individuals, but between entire nations. This reality is clearly seen through the history of humanity, where a devastating trail of wars, atrocities, and human genocide reflect our attempts to control and dominate others.

However, when we look at life with the mindset of—What does God think or say about me or this person—everything changes. What are God's plans and purposes as opposed to my limited outlook? What is God's heart and perspective about a matter? Codependency and self-focused independence can be replaced by life-giving interdependency and dependency on God. Codependency is an excessive reliance on other people for approval and a sense of identity. God-dependence is the birthplace of a rich love that can empower friendships, family, and intimate relationships. It's not easy, but it is possible to experience a freedom from self-seeking, as we embark on a journey of surrender, enabled by the Holy Spirit. In the ensuing chapters, we will explore the practical ways in which we can be released from our brokenness.

A few years ago, we were flying home from a ministry engagement on Southwest Airlines and failed to check in early enough to get a boarding position. As a member of the late numbered "C" group, we were feeling flustered in the very back of the plane. Soon after takeoff, there were a couple of infants at the front of the plane who started screaming and didn't end until the flight landed. From our vantage point, we could see that the passengers up front were clearly irritated by the commotion. Yet, sitting in the very back, we had the advantage of being insulated from all of the noise. At that very moment, we realized that our oversight actually turned out to be a blessing. If we had only just rested in the providence of our situation, we wouldn't have been so stressed or agitated over our situation in the first place.

Rather than complaining or accusing each other with "You should have!" "Why didn't you?" "If only…" or any other "What ifs?" we could have rested in the "God's got this" perspective. Letting go is a lifelong journey that will ease the tension of life's many inconveniences and disturbances. And sometimes our little annoyances can become a blessing in disguise. On that fateful flight, Jesus' words came to mind that indeed, "the last shall be first, and the first last."[6]

Reflect-Respond-Renew

_____

[6] Matthew 20:16 (NKJV)

Take a moment to answer a few questions that will help you recognize some of the ways in which control hides itself in your actions. If you answer yes to more than five questions, chances are, you struggle with control in some areas. In the spirit of full transparency, both of us have responded yes to many more than five!

1. Do you tend to want to correct others and tell them the "right" way to do something?
2. Do you tend to be the leader in situations or to generally be in charge?
3. Do you want to be the one who explains instructions and /or directions?
4. Do you correct others when they are talking if they have the information wrong or incomplete?
5. Do you find yourself interrupting conversations to give your input or opinion?
6. Do you worry about things on a regular basis?
7. Do you tend to "one-up" (elevate yourself) above others in social situations?
8. Are you a fearful or insecure person?
9. Do you generally not trust people?
10. Do you think you are right most of the time?

11. Are you a back-seat driver?
12. Are you overly involved in family members' lives?
13. Are you constantly trying to figure out and problem-solve for yourself and others?
14. Can you see any me-centeredness view in your answers to the questions above?
15. At times you struggle to fully believe that God has control over all things in your life?

Chapter Three
Hurts That Need Healing

At the core of every individual is a desire to love and to be loved. As children, we become aware of approval and disapproval, acceptance and rejection through something as simple as an unkind word from a classmate or an adult who spoke harshly to us for doing something wrong. Wounds like these cause us to question our self-worth and confidence. These memories can easily linger for years or even decades, affecting our life, identity, and relationships. Love can only flourish in an environment of trust and safety. So, when we are hurt by others, we naturally develop defenses to protect ourselves and many of these coping tactics can be unhealthy.

The echoes of childhood wounds can linger for a lifetime. When I (Mickey) was around eleven-years-old, I distinctly remember a day that changed my life for years to come. It was a rainy-day schedule in my sixth-grade class. At lunchtime, our teacher led us in a number of indoor classroom games. One of the games was Twenty Questions. In this game, a student went outside of the classroom while the teacher picked an object in the room. When the student reentered the classroom, he or she had twenty guesses to identify the chosen object. During one of the rounds, the teacher had chosen as the object a hair comb that was sticking out of my top shirt pocket. As you can imagine, being a preadolescent, I was already a bit self-conscious about being the center of attention. As the game continued, my classmate successfully narrowed down within a dozen questions that the object had something to do with me. His next question shattered me for years: "Is it Mickey's buck teeth?" The class erupted in laughter, and at that moment I died inside.

I didn't even know I had buck teeth. But once my classmate said that I did, dark thoughts took root in my heart. I started telling myself terrible things, like, "I am ugly. I am dumb." All of my childhood pictures from that moment on showed me with a closed-mouthed smile. I never wanted to reveal my "bucked teeth" ever again. I begged my parents for braces. Insecurity grew and the lies about my self-worth began dominating my thinking and identity.

As noted in Genesis chapters 1-2, humanity was created in God's image, and Adam and Eve lived in harmony with God and each other. This is what we call the "true self." It is who God intended us to be. Love, mutuality, friendship, security, and intimacy were meant to be dominant in the human experience. But sadly, chapter three of Genesis entered into our narrative. It was there that the "fallen self" was governed by sin, death, blame, shame, and pride. And as a result of our fallen human nature, sin multiplies as we interact with others, hurting and wounding more people by the moment. This becomes the realm where fear, errant identities, lies, toxic thoughts, and demonic influences disrupt our love and unity. At this point, it is natural for wounded individuals to self-protect in order to avoid further trauma. Sadly, however, we often use unhealthy coping mechanisms to guard against being hurt any further.

My "pseudo-self" assumed the protective mantle of humor. After that incident in class, I would do anything to get a laugh. I realized that if I could get people to laugh with me, I wouldn't necessarily feel that they were laughing at me. I became the class clown, so much so that I earned that superlative in my high school senior yearbook. But deep inside, I was still an insecure eleven-year-old that hid his pain behind a mask of humor.

There are countless stories that replicate this narrative—it isn't special or unique in any way. Young, insecure, and vulnerable children, teenagers, and adults walk through social situations like this every day. Do you remember what it was like to be that person who was the brunt of another's cruel comment? Your first experience with woundedness may not have been rejection from a friend. It may have been caused by your parents' divorce, someone else's rage, your older brother's drug addiction, or the death of a loved one that left you feeling lost, lonely, confused, unwanted, and fearful. Not all of us walk away with deep wounds from these types of incidents, but many of us often do. Wounds can trigger us throughout our lives, consciously or unconsciously, due to early experiences of rejection. Insecurity, fear, pain, and uncertainty can rule our interactions with others, and guardedness becomes our default.

This is where control comes into play. We find ourselves in everyday situations at work, home, or social settings, unaware of the fact that we are attempting to control the environment and/or a situation we're in. And we're doing it all in a subconscious effort to protect ourselves from wounds inflicted long ago.

Imagine for a moment if control was a person, and everywhere he or she went they felt the need to assert their sovereignty. They put up walls and barricades, only letting people in on their own terms. The person calls to mind every rejection and wound in their soul, and posts on every entryway for all to read, "Enter at your own risk." It's like when we put a smile on our face, but inside we could be feeling angry, sad, or lonely.

Control believes that self-protection is the safest place to hide and always stays on the defensive, even when doing so traps the controller in a cold and lonely existence. Control pushes others away and subconsciously creates barriers to guard against potential pain. It avoids vulnerability and seeks to manipulate others, in an effort to shut down every potential offender. Control tells us that this is a much easier path than dealing with more pain and that by manipulating situations, circumstances, and relationships, we can have the upper hand. Isolation and withdrawal are its rearguard. Pride is its shield. In its defensiveness, control tells us the lie that we can't trust anybody but ourselves. We might find ourselves saying, "I'm fine, I'll do it myself. I don't need anybody."

C. S. Lewis addressed this tendency when discussing the nature of love's vulnerability to pain. It's scary to let go, but the alternative is far worse:

> "Love anything, and your heart will certainly be wrung, possibly be broken. If you want to make sure of keeping it intact, you must give your heart to no one, not even to an animal. Wrap it carefully around with hobbies and little luxuries; avoid all entanglements; lock it up safe in the casket or coffin of your selfishness. But in that casket—safe, dark, motionless, airless—it will not change. It will not be broken; it will become unbreakable, impenetrable, irredeemable. The alternative to tragedy, or at least to the risk of tragedy, is damnation. The only place outside of heaven where you can be perfectly safe from all the dangers and perturbations of love is hell."[7]

Loving something or someone necessarily opens our heart to the likelihood of being hurt. This does not mean that we should be defenseless against abuse or enable another's bad behavior. But it does mean that we have to allow ourselves exposure to potential pain, in order to

---

[7] Lewis C. S. (1960). *The Four Loves.* San Francisco, CA: Harper One.

experience true love. Though seemingly paradoxical, vulnerability is a pathway to freedom.

An ally of control is his good friend, narcissism. Narcissism embodies a grandiose sense of self-importance and lacks empathy for others given its self-focus. But what many fail to recognize is that narcissism, at its core, manifests most often as wounded children seeking to guard themselves at all cost. A true narcissist can't see his or her own self-focus, which skews their perception of reality. Narcissists actually identify narcissism in others, when in fact, they are merely projecting a mirror image of their duplicity for self-protection. So, if a number of people come to mind that you consider to be narcissists, then take heed—the real narcissist just might be you!

Control often causes us to run away from others while peeking in the rearview mirror, hoping that someone cares enough to chase us. Ironically, control makes us afraid of being vulnerable but causes us to crave transparency in others. Controlling people want to connect, but sabotage opportunities to do so. They want to feel safe enough to let go but rarely release the reins enough to see if that's even possible. Controlling people lack trust, which is essential to experiencing true intimacy and love in our closest relationships.

Control never makes us feel safe and is rarely without anxiety. At the foundation of trust is the need for authentic faith. It seems counterintuitive to controlling people that in order to experience freedom from the pain of our past, we must give up control. Letting go, being vulnerable, and allowing people to know us requires a huge leap of faith. Faith turns vulnerability into freedom and transforms trust into intimacy. True freedom is rooted in faith in the God of love. It is His love and perspective that work in us to restore us into our original design.

Dr. Brené Brown, a research professor at the University of Houston Graduate College of Social Work, has spent the past decade investigating two topics that feed directly into our desire to control: vulnerability and shame. Relinquishing control requires us to trust others and to ultimately trust God. When we do, we allow ourselves to become exposed (vulnerable), wherein the lies of shame are uncovered, unshackling the weight of self-absorbed defensiveness. Dr. Brown astutely affirms that "we need to feel trust to be vulnerable and we need to be vulnerable in order to trust."[8] In other words, freedom from self is where we discover freedom for self.

Control and surrender reminds us of the age-old "chicken-or-the-egg" debate—which came first? We would venture to say that the same concept applies to our wrestling with control and surrender. We have to release control in order to experience surrender, but we have to surrender in order to experience a release from control. Herein lies the freedom that allows us to live a life full of grace. But either way you cut it, this is a risky position for the wounded. And as for those wounds, we

---

[8] Brown, C. Brene. (2015). *Daring Greatly: How the Courage to Be Vulnerable Transforms the Way We Live, Love, Parent, and Lead.* New York, New York: Avery Publishing.

would not love you well if we did not address this subject again, directly and relentlessly. Here's why: our wounds are what holds us back. They keep us hostage to the full freedom that is found in letting go. We all believe that forgiveness is critical to the process of healing. But you might be wondering, "What is forgiveness, really?"

Forgiveness, at its root, is grounded solely in the forgiveness we have received from God through Jesus Christ. In Christ, we experience forgiveness from our sin and brokenness. God forgives all who call upon Him and then empowers His followers to forgive others. We can only forgive others, because we, ourselves have been forgiven. Forgiveness is rooted in forgiven-ness. Ephesians 4:31-32 instructs us to, "let all bitterness, wrath, anger, clamor, and evil speaking be put away from you, with all malice. And be kind to one another, tenderhearted, forgiving one another, even as God in Christ forgave you." As we forgive others, the bitterness for the wrong has no more power over us and we are free to trust again. This is a process that can take time.

Our wounds may run deep, but it is possible to begin trusting others again and to let go of self-defensiveness. Faith in Jesus Christ literally empowers His followers to experience unconditional acceptance that enables us to become vulnerable and trusting. To know that we are loved and accepted by God becomes the lens through which all other relationships are understood. To feel safe is to know that God is always present, and sovereignly working through the circumstances of our lives for a higher and better

35

purpose. This truth can set us free, by helping us realize that there is a bigger plan, even in our pain. That may sound a bit cliché, but when you reflect on God's goodness, you will begin to grasp His truth that surrendering to ultimate love helps us relinquish our need to control.

Reflect-Respond-Renew

As we begin to explore our feelings, wounds, and responses, we can start to examine our emotions, thoughts, and behaviors. Controlling, excusing, and blaming others are some of the by-products of self-preservation, pride, and narcissism. Herein lies another key in moving towards healing and freedom: self-examination and feedback from others. Prioritizing the choice to be honest with ourselves and recognizing why we do what we do and say, can help us begin to discern the trigger of our actions, and our need to control. This is where the Biblical truth of what God declares about us is so very critical. When we believe this truth, we replace the deception of our shame with God's love and acceptance. Below are a number of ways to begin to grow in this area.

1.) Identifying behaviors and motives. Reflect on the following questions:

- What circumstances have triggered feelings of insecurity, rejection, trust, fear, and pride?
- If I'm honest with my motives, what actions of control (manipulation, guilting, shaming, criticizing) have I displayed with others for self-protection?
- What is one thing I can identify in how I am feeling that is hindering me

from letting go of my manipulation of others?
- Does this current scenario remind me of a past hurt from which I've developed defensiveness?
- Is there someone I need to forgive?
- Take time to write out your thoughts in a journal.

2) Believe the Biblical truths of what God affirms of His children in the Bible:
- I am loved (John 3:16).
- I am forgiven (1 John 1:9).
- I am approved (2 Timothy 2:15).
- I am accepted (Acts 10:35).
- I am the apple of His eye (Deuteronomy 32:10).
- I am an overcomer (1 John 5:4).
- I am free (Luke 4:18).
- I am His beloved (Psalm 127:2).
- I have power over fear (1 Timothy1:7).

3) Action steps:
- Commit to seeing a counselor, mentor, or pastor who will guide you in your personal growth through past wounds.
- What is a healthier way to cope when I feel criticized or rejected?

- What can I change or do differently when a similar circumstance arises?
- What are the steps I need to take to grow my trust in God for this area?
- Look for one situation this week where you hold your tongue and don't give your input or suggestions with a family member or friend. (It may be a small thing or a major one.) Say a prayer over the situation and give it to God. Let go!
- Memorize this promise of God: "Fear not, for I am with you; be not dismayed, for I am your God. I will strengthen you, yes, I will help you, I will uphold you with My righteous right hand."[9]

---

[9] Isaiah 41:10 (NKJV).

Chapter Four
Right, Wrong or Just Different?

A very famous pop song came out in 2001, and the chorus to it went, "All the women, who are independent—throw your hands up at me."[10] Let me (Karen) be the first to throw my hands up high! Growing up in the middle of a large dysfunctional family (as most of us do), I became quite skilled in fending for myself and getting things done. I also prided myself in being that independent woman who doesn't need help or input from anyone. After all, I had been doing just fine by myself for years. As such, the seed of needing to be right and in control blossomed deep down in my heart at a young age. Then I fell in love ... yikes! Being married reveals all sorts of things you never knew about yourself.

It didn't take long in sharing my life so closely with someone else to recognize this independence thing went way deeper than I thought. As I began to take the risk of looking into the recesses of my heart, I found my need to control glaring at me. I had created the illusion that my way was right, and anything else was just plain wrong. After all, being independent entitles you to see yourself as the captain of your own soul. Once again, I learned a great lesson in self-awareness when I strongly directed my husband that he was washing the dishes

---

[10] *Independent Women,* Destiny's Child, Songwriters: Mark Rooney, Samuel Barnes, Jean Olivier, and Beyoncé Knowles, Sony/ATV Music Publishing LLC, Warner Chappell Music, Inc, Songtrust Ave

wrong! Were they getting clean? Yes. Was he breaking any dishes in the process? No. But it wasn't how I would wash the dishes; so clearly his way just wouldn't work for me. He was doing a helpful chore, that many wives would appreciate. Yet, it wasn't my way of doing things, so I couldn't appreciate him for trying to pitch in.

A good friend shared her similar story about the first time she went camping with her husband. She had asked him to be in charge of starting the fire. Instead of her unpacking the car as she intended, she found herself standing close by and telling him the right way to start a fire! His tepee method was not working (at least in her estimation), so she directed him as to how it was to be done. It was her way or the highway! She told her husband to go unpack the car and she'd start the fire. But wait, she thought, he might not do that right either! Her conclusion was that he should just sit down and let her do it all, which was absolutely ridiculous, but that's the thing about control. It will scream the lie that life is black and white. In the controlling person's mind, there is a right way (my way) and there is a wrong way (any other way). There is no middle ground. A world of hurt gathers at the feet of this deception.

I've seen this I'm right, you're wrong thing play out in more than just the context of marriages. It sneaks into the workplace, where we can find it difficult to delicate tasks to others. That's because, in our minds, we tell ourselves that letting someone else assume responsibility for a task would be a bad idea because we can do it better. That false conclusion burdens us with additional responsibilities and robs others of the chance to build their own self-confidence. This outcome makes both parties miserable, but how do we break this destructive cycle, fueled by the desire to control?

We start by asking ourselves the following questions whether at home or work, "Will the end results be the same? Will the dishes be clean? Will there be a fire to sit by when the sun goes down? In other words, if we just ask whether the job will get done, we'll realize that yes, it will—without our interference! There is so much liberty in realizing that everything doesn't have to be a struggle or fight. Different ways of approaching tasks and problems can simply be that—different! And different isn't bad. Control tells us different is dangerous because our way is the only "right" way. But that lie is exposed by the beauty of compromise, which invites love into every interaction. Biblical love, which frees us from fear, is always the best response to control's manipulative lies. When Jesus' followers asked Him what was the most important thing they could do, His answer was simply, "Love God and love people." Everything boils down to love, which means thinking of others before yourself, putting their needs before yours, and yes, even preferring their ways to yours.

We see Jesus as the perfect example of what love looks like. When Jesus gave up His rights, He also let go of any entitlements as He surrendered to the will of His Father. In other words, He humbled Himself to show the world true love shows preference to others. When you pause to ask and listen, God tenderly whispers His truth into all of life's circumstances. It's not a right versus wrong; me versus you thing. There's just a hallowed ground we can embrace called "different," upon which love, grace, and freedom are found. People should always be prioritized over a task. This is where we have the choice to see things our way or through the lens of God's love for others. What a great challenge for us to surrender to God's perspective of love and to see things from another's point of view. Seeking to understand more than to be understood, is central to God's definition of love. Our goal should be to value all that people offer us with the heart of our loving Father. This makes letting go a joy rather than a duty, and the fruit of such a heart will bring growth and peace in your relationships. Right relationships are almost always more important than being right.

Years ago, I (Mickey) was honored to perform the wedding ceremony of a San Diego firefighter couple. The ceremony was all planned out in great detail and took place outside in beautiful Balboa Park. My job was to follow their planned script for their wedding and to incorporate all of their many particulars, to which I willingly obliged. As a pastor you learn the principle, "what the bride wants, the bride gets." At the close of the ceremony, the couple wanted to release doves as a symbol of their freedom to soar in their new love together. To save a little money, the groom went to a local pet store and bought two domesticated doves. The option of hiring a dove keeper with trained doves is, of course, a bit pricier.

The wedding went off without a hitch and all was very honoring to the couple's plans until the final release of the doves. I opened the cage and one at a time I delivered the two doves to the bride and groom. Then together, they lifted up the doves to release them into their new-found freedom. Perhaps because they were domesticated and had never flown in the wild, the two doves were somewhat confused. One flew horizontally a few feet above the ground until it slammed head-first into a wall. The other dove clutched the arbor just a couple of feet overhead. As a symbol, I thought that this wasn't a very promising way to start a marriage, so I took action to give this part of the ceremony a second try. With the help of the groom, we gathered to two dazed doves and the couple repeated the release with an even more drastic result. Let's just say that it didn't go well for the feathered friends. The remarkable part of the story, however, wasn't what happened with the doves (may they rest in peace). What caught my attention was how this couple turned a fowl experience, into an experience of levity. Rather than being frustrated over their plans that went awry, they laughed together, which freed their wedding guests to do the same. This couple had learned the secret to contentment on day-one of their marriage; letting go of control, and laughing at "different" outcomes whenever possible. What a great example of how to live life for the rest of us!

Reflect-Respond-Renew

1) Identifying behaviors and motives. Reflect on the following questions. As you ponder these questions, seek to have an honest awareness of your feelings and attitudes.

- Are there any areas in my life where I need to have things done my way? Why do I feel this? What negative emotion is it triggering?
- In what relationships do I find myself creating the barrier or need to be right, at the expense of relational harmony?
- What type of control am I using? Manipulation, guilt, shame, criticism, or pride?
- Why am I afraid of letting go of my way or perspective?
- Do I tend to seek to understand others and to let others do things their way?
- Does a current scenario remind me of a past hurt from which I've developed defenses or patterns?
- Could my actions simply be selfish?

2) Believe the Biblical truths of what God affirms of His children in the Bible:

- "Be kindly affectionate to one another with brotherly love, in honor giving preference to one another" (Romans 12:10 NKJV).
- "Let this mind be in you, which was also in Christ Jesus, Who, being in the form of God, thought it not robbery to be equal with God, but made Himself of no reputation, and took on Him the form of a servant, and was made in the likeness of men. And being found in fashion as a man, He humbled Himself, and became obedient to the point of death, even the death of the cross" (Philippians 2:5-8 NKJV).
- "The greatest in God's Kingdom is the servant of all" (Matthew 18:4 NKJV).

3) Action Steps:

- Think of a pleasant response you can say when you don't agree with someone. A response that will help build unity. For example, "I can see why you think that or why you would do it that way." Practice active listening to truly value the person you are with. Seeking to understand them shows them value. As you listen to others, think to yourself, "This is the most important person in the world to me right now."

- Try and put yourself in the other person's shoes; how that person may feel when there is a difference or disagreement. Seek to be attentive to their feelings as well.
- How would Jesus handle this situation?
- Memorize one of the promises above and say it out loud throughout the day.
- Read Galatians 5 today. Ask for God to fill you with His Spirit and seek to see others through His heart.

Chapter Five
The Pain of Our Pride

We all have painful stories of broken relationships. Some are more devastating than others. It's ironic that, at times, our pain is a result of our own actions. The Bible warns us that sometimes challenges come our way as a direct result of our own doings. We often reap what we have sown. When we plant seeds of pride, it can bear the fruit of discord in relationships. At the root of so many of life's most painful wounds, the cancer of a prideful ego can influence our interactions to our own demise.

I (Karen) grew up in a family of seven kids, and as you might expect, conflict was common. However, one of the most hurtful memories that comes to mind was the ongoing strife between one of my brothers and my father. Their non-stop friction became a tutorial for future generations on the pain of our pride. Both are amazing men, intelligent, caring, with hearts of gold – yet both are full of pride. My father was a self-made, hardworking entrepreneur, who was a know-it-all who took a lot of pride in his work. He was a staunch conservative from the Greatest Generation and was raised during the Great Depression, where jobs were few and times were hard. His father was very tough on him, with high expectations and a constant push for more. As a result, most anything my father did, he did with excellence and he took great pride in his accomplishments. The need for affirmation and value from my grandfather fueled much of my dad's ambition. And as history so often repeats itself, my dad was the same way with his sons. My dad's name is Ken, and his firstborn son was also named Ken. Sadly, my oldest brother couldn't possibly live up to my father's expectations.

I'm sure this story is repeated in many other families—a father who's married to his work, and a son who never saw or felt valued by his dad. My dad never showed love or affirmation for his son. In some ways, they were mirror images and polar opposites of each other. My brother was free-spirited, adventurous, born in the '50s and lived like most teenagers did during the '70s. Ken Jr.'s perspective was more liberal and embraced the culture of his era. As far back as I can remember, my brother loved to argue. He eventually became the president of his high school's debate team. He was quick, intelligent, and quite the philosopher.

As you might imagine, my dad also liked to be right and as a result of their ongoing arguments, my father and brother eventually grew apart. Towards the end of my father's life, there was an explosive interaction between the two over politics. At least five years went by, including birthdays and holidays, with no communication between them. Although my brother made several attempts to contact our father and make amends, all attempts proved unsuccessful. This narrative is sadly common in families with wounds. So how do we mend these relationships? Who makes the first call, when both parties feel as though they have been wronged?

What if one party doesn't want to reconcile? Deep-rooted disagreements often grow out of undetected pain in our hearts. When two wounded souls both believe that their perspective of an issue is right, both are blinded by their egos. Ultimately, pride builds a wall that serves as a fortress against love, reconciliation, and reason. Pride prevents us from seeing things from another's perspective. Pride says, "I am right, and you're wrong!" Pride also can be a disguise to self-protect when one's worldview is believed to be under attack. When someone's self-worth is tied to a need to be right, control finds an opportunity to sneak in to derail the relationship.

A number of years later my brother was diagnosed with throat cancer which led to a very painful season of surgeries, radiation, and chemotherapy. As my father came to the realization that he was on the verge of losing his son, grace entered their relationship, as pride and control fell away. Cancer and possibility of death brought these two strong-willed, though God-fearing men, closer to one another. Fortunately, a miraculous shift came as a result of one of my brother's chemotherapy treatments. Weak and somewhat tortured by the chemicals in his body, he drifted off into a dream or vision that transformed his perception of his father. His eyes were open, but in his mind's eye, he saw our father gliding down an enormous slide; the kind you see at a waterslide park. His father's face was full of joy and laughter. My brother could see a childlikeness in his dad's face as he was having the time of his life. At that

God used cancer to bring about change

moment, God spoke to my brother's heart and said, "This is who I meant for your dad to be."

Suddenly, my brother was flooded with so much love for our dad. As he saw Dad through God's eyes, instead of through the eyes of pain and rejection, his heart changed toward him. In that moment, God began a healing work and nurtured a new understanding to his heart. This revelation of who God created our father to be dissolved years of bitter conflict between them. By seeing our father through the eyes of God, my brother was freed from his own pride and pain, which enabled him to experience freedom from needing to be right and to be in control of their relationship.

In his work, The Weight of Glory, C. S. Lewis made this incredible declaration:

> "It is a serious thing to live in a society of possible gods and goddesses, to remember that the dullest most uninteresting person you can talk to may one day be a creature which, if you saw it now, you would be strongly tempted to worship… it is with the awe and the circumspection proper to them, that we should conduct all of our dealings with one another, all friendships, all loves, all play, all politics. There are no ordinary people. You have never talked to a mere mortal. Nations, cultures, arts, civilizations - these are mortal, and their life is to ours as the life of a gnat. But it is

immortals whom we joke with, work with, marry, snub, and exploit."[11]

Imagine if we could see each other in faith as God sees His children! As Lewis says, we would be tempted to worship one another. It is that perspective of honor (short of actual worship of course), that nurtures the grace in us to humbly let our guards down, and forgive as God forgives.   Amen

Let's further dissect pride for a moment. The need to self-exalt and to self-protect are often closely aligned. Pride calls attention to self and elevates one's own worth, often at the expense of others. At the heart of this is a deep need to feel safe. Ironically, arrogance can stem from a poor self-image, which triggers the need to have others believe we have value and worth. What's more, the need to elevate the ego can directly influence our relationships negatively to our own detriment. Pride is often the blind spot lurking deep down in our character that builds a fortress against vulnerability and transparency. In an attempt to avoid discomfort, our woundedness can elevate the craving of the ego to the point of sabotaging our own self-worth.

In his classic work, Humility, Andrew Murray wrote, "Let us, at the very beginning of our meditations, admit that there is nothing so natural to man, nothing so subtle and hidden from our sight, nothing so difficult and dangerous, as pride."[12] It is outrageous that the need to

---

[11] Lewis, C.S. (2001). *Weight of Glory.* San Francisco, CA: HarperOne.

feel safe can be the hidden motive that becomes a source for further pain. The truth is, there is only One who is always right; God Almighty. Jesus made this reality crystal clear when He asserted that He is the way, the truth, and the life. His perspectives, as revealed in the Scriptures, are the starting point for bringing harmony with one's self and others.

As we navigate our relationships, cognizant of the fact that we all have painful baggage from our past, there is such freedom in letting go of the ego of self-protection. It is actually possible to let go and to engage others through the lens of God's truth. Only then will we be able to see people as they truly are; perfectly made in the image of God. This necessitates greater self-awareness to our own motives and triggers, as we slow down to actively listen and understand another's point of view. Admitting our own brokenness and choosing humility, forgiveness, and grace can help restore our true identity and bring healing to our relationships. It is in humility and surrender that we allow God, freedom to be in control. The truth is, if you ever think you've arrived at being humble, you'll realize that your pride is showing off again.

---

[12] Murray, Andrew. ((1982). *Humility.* New Kensington, PA: Whitaker House.

Reflect-Respond-Renew

1) Identifying behaviors and motives. Reflect on the following questions. As you ponder these questions, seek to have an honest awareness of your feelings and attitudes.

- What area in my life do I most feel the need to be right?
- Do I have insecurity or trust issues from past rejections that I can identify?
- In your interactions with others, at times do you find yourself manipulating, guilting, shaming, or criticizing?

2) Believe the Biblical truths of what God affirms of His children in the Bible:

- "Humble yourselves in the sight of the Lord, and He will lift you up" (James 4:10 NKJV).
- "Do nothing out of selfish ambition or vain conceit. Rather, in humility value others above yourselves, not looking to your own interests but each of you to the interests of the others" (Philippians 2:3-4 NKJV).
- "Trust in the Lord with all your heart, and lean not on your own understanding; in all your ways

acknowledge Him, and He shall direct your paths. Do not be wise in your own eyes; fear the Lord and depart from evil" (Proverbs 3:5-7 NKJV).

- "The wicked in his pride does not seek God. God is in none of his thoughts" (Psalm 10:4 NKJV).
- "The fear of the Lord is to hate evil; Pride and arrogance and the evil way and the perverse mouth I hate" (Proverbs 8:13 NKJV).

3) Action Steps:

- Ask the Lord to open your eyes to focus on loving people and seeing them the way He does, rather than on your need to be right.
- Memorize one of the promises of God above and say it out loud throughout the day.
- Look for one situation where you hold your tongue, wherein you would normally try to "one-up" another person. "One up" is a term used to identify how we will say something that makes us look better than the other person. Say a prayer over the

situation and give it to God and let go.

The act of love is laying down oneself and opinions to prefer another above yourself. It is unimaginable to grasp the fact that the Father gave His Son, Jesus, that we might have a personal relationship with God. Let us follow His example and lay down our lives and opinions for others. Humility, true gospel humility, means I stop connecting every experience and every conversation for my own benefit. In fact, I stop thinking about myself. There is freedom in self-forgetfulness. There is a blessed rest that only self-forgetfulness brings.

Chapter Six
The Great Façade

We can finally now say that we are officially classic (in other words, "old"- though aged in years, not in heart and attitude). We are both in our sixties and have been married for over forty blessed years. We have an awesome marriage—not a perfect marriage, but a relationship that is continually growing more enjoyable every day. For nearly four decades, we have worked together to invest our hearts, minds, and souls into improving our relationship. There have been many successes and achievements, but there have also been many misunderstandings and painful challenges along the way. God has been faithful to uncover deep-rooted seeds of control that have been barriers to our much-needed growth.

Control disguises itself from our radar as it lurks on the edges, and hides beneath the surface of our intentions and motives. Whenever the topic of control is brought up, there's a tendency to put up the wall and silently utter, "Surely that's not me." This struggle is not something we have overcome, but it is a nemesis that requires a daily reliance on God's help for change.

I (Karen) remember the day well; it was early afternoon in December. The kids were all in school and Mickey was home on his day off. I had gone to the mailbox, eagerly looking for Christmas cards and anything that didn't resemble a bill. There it was: a card from my dad. Every year he sent money to us for

Christmas. You need to know, at this time I was a stay at home mom with four little kids attending a private school on a Pastor's salary. We barely made ends meet each month. I often shopped at second-hand clothing stores and garage sales. That Christmas money was a big bonus for us. You would think getting money would be something to celebrate, but that is not what happened that day. As I read the amount of the check to Mickey with great excitement, he said: "we need to save that." "No," I blurted out, "we are going to spend it for Christmas!" After all, it came from my father, not his, and I felt like I had a legitimate say in how it should be used. It's funny how something as good as receiving a gift can become a trigger to assert control.

Years later, my sister pointed out my controlling nature. I remember the night well. It was a lovely summer evening, and my family was preparing dinner together. I gave my husband the task of cutting vegetables to prepare for grilling. I was getting other items ready when I looked over and saw that he was cutting the vegetables the wrong way. I felt that they were too small for the barbecue and that they would fall through the grill. I wanted to help him, by showing him the right way to cut vegetables. "Here, let me help you, honey," I said. "I got it," he quickly shot back. Okay, no big deal I thought—whatever. It wasn't until later that evening that my sister, who was visiting, pointed out to me what she had observed regarding our interactions in the kitchen. I wouldn't have seen my suggestion to him as control. I thought I was just helping him. But if you asked my husband if I was being overly "helping" (controlling), I am pretty sure he would have said yes.

At this point you might be thinking, isn't that a bit petty? Well, let's stop and think it through. Have you ever found yourself saying to a completely capable person, "Let me help you with that?" Or perhaps you suggested to someone, "You should do it like this. This way is better, faster and easier." In an attempt to help others, we sometimes inadvertently elevate our way of doing things over theirs. Our helping oftentimes isn't really coming alongside others to assist, but instead, an attempt to show others the way it should be done from our perspective. Most often it isn't a case of wrong or right but of personal preference. Oh, how invisible these blind spots can be!

By choice, I was a stay-at-home mom and ran the household. I was the one that taught the kids how to do things while my husband was working. I was with our children a majority of the time. My playbook at the house was the one that we needed to use. I had a full-time job at home which included the kids' homework, preparing meals, getting to sports practice, and a variety of other commitments. Ultimately, I didn't want my husband to tell me how to do my job. When he was home, he loved to come up with spontaneous outings to mix it up and have a little fun. These ideas just didn't fit in with my routines. If I was in control and things were done my way, then my world would be safe and I could avoid uncomfortable and anxious feelings that come from the unexpected. His spontaneity was unsettling to the tranquility I'd worked so hard to establish at home.[13]

There are a number of issues that fuel our bossiness, and an ongoing need for self-reflection to examine our motives and reactions to situations that are out of our control. It is essential to develop honest and transparent relationships amongst trusted mentors, friends, and family members where we can be vulnerable and accountable for our emotional triggers. These can become intentional relationships where change and freedom can grow. The help of an effective Christian counselor is also another recommended option for assistance. However, the utmost encouragement in Scripture is that we would make it our priority to seek God's wisdom and perspective as He is our wonderful Counselor and Father.

God is present and attentive to our inquiries every hour of the day. As we pursue Him in His Word and spend time with Him in prayer, God is able to reveal to us our struggles and the hidden parts of our hearts. In the Gospel of John 8:31-32, Jesus said to the Jews who believed in Him, "If you abide in My Word, you are My disciples indeed. And you shall know the truth and the truth shall make you free" (NKJV). God's heart for us is to set us free from the lies and wounds that uproot our peace, love, and joy. He desires for us to have a life that is free from worry and the need to control. At

---

[13] For a related blog resource for enrichment go to:
https://www.symbis.com/blog/10-ways-to-let-go-of-control-in-your-marriage/?mc_cid=103dd66e2e&mc_eid=48d16135a0

our core, we desire freedom from the prison of being controlled. Yet, to accomplish this, we often seek to control others. How deceptive is that!

Whatever our excuses maybe for "helping" others, the bottom line is that we need to grow in the contentment of letting go, which allows others to do things the way they prefer to. Now there are times, of course, when others ask for our genuine input and we should respond with humility and grace. In other words, we are allowed to have opinions! We just need to be guarded against forcing our ways on to others when it comes to our preferences. Jesus is waiting to be with us each morning as the day dawns and we open our eyes to a new beginning. His arms are wide open and His heart is full of love for us as He seeks to grow our relationship with Him. Be free to tell Him what is on your mind and share your concerns and burdens. Tell Jesus how much you love Him and need Him to guard your heart to live out His preferences—not yours. Follow Jesus' example in praying, "Father… not My will, but Yours be done."[14] Ask God for His presence to be with you as you go about your day. Your intimacy with God is the key to letting go and trusting Him with the outcome of every situation.

The preeminent good in any circumstance is God's perspective. Since God is love (1 John 4:7), the ultimate help for others is to invite His love into every situation. Before we say or do anything for another person, ask yourself if your motivation is to build them

---

[14] John 8:31,32 (NKJV).

up in love or to have your way. Even if you lose a few vegetables through the grill, it's worth the freedom you'll find in letting go!

Reflect-Respond-Renew

1) Identifying behaviors and motives. Reflect on the following questions:

- What sensitive areas have been resurfacing as a trigger for me? (E.g. Insecurity, rejection, trust issues, fear, pride, past trauma, a need to be loved or accepted.)
- What type of control am I using in these situations? Am I manipulating, guilting, criticizing or arrogant in my responses and interactions?
- What is stopping me from letting go of my need to control others? Is it pride or the need to be right, or wanting my way?
- Do my current circumstances remind me of a past hurt from which I've developed defenses or controlling patterns?

2) Believe the Biblical truths of what God affirms of His children in the Bible:

- Jesus is my Helper (John 14:16).
- God is my defender (Psalm 59:16)
- Jesus will never leave me (Hebrews 13:5).
- Jesus only loves me with an everlasting love (Jeremiah 31:3).
- I am an overcomer (1 John 5:4).
- God will perfect that which concerns me (Psalm 138:8).

3) Action Steps:

- What can I change or do differently the next time I'm in a similar circumstance?
- How do I want to respond or feel in the situation?
- Look for a situation this week where you would normally give your opinion or suggestion to a coworker, family member, or roommate. Instead of giving your opinion, make it a priority to understand others and to ask for their perspective. Seek to see things from another point of view first.

Memorize one of the promises of God listed above and say it out loud throughout the day. Read Philippians chapter 2 and meditate on Jesus Christ's humility. Remember to "Let nothing be done through selfish ambition or conceit, but in lowliness of mind let each esteem others better than himself. Let each of you look out not only for his own interests, but also for the interests of others."[15]

[15] Philippians 2:3, 4 (NKJV)

Chapter Seven
Freedom from Self

How, where, and when we grow up in our family of origin has a significant influence on who we become as adults. There are a variety of factors that can play into this reality. There is also a plethora of research on the impact of family dynamics on human development. The crazy thing about our families is that not one of us ever had the option to choose our family of origin. They are the soil in which we have been planted, and it is in our homes where we begin to develop many of our perspectives on life, including our coping skills for navigating relationships. Our social upbringing creates an environment where love, safety, and trust can be nurtured or neglected. Our beginnings are also where we learn to look out for ourselves and, if necessary, to defend ourselves at all costs.

For me (Karen), growing up in a blended family of nine people taught me the selfless quality of considering others before myself. I had six other siblings to contend with for time, space, food, and attention. You can't even imagine the energy, activity, and shenanigans that occurred on an average day. I am right in the middle of the pack; three older and three younger. My parents started having kids when they were in high school. They had five children in seven short years. Divorce came, followed by remarriages, which brought into our lives a stepmom and a stepsister close to my age. Later, one more girl was born into our expanding family. All that to say, seven kids under one roof in the space of nine years was pretty wild!

With both parents working full time and disengaged from their children, we were unsupervised most of the time. As such, the survival instinct built the need to be attentive to any potential threat that could influence my safety. I grew up very aware of others' opinions, wants, preferences, and needs. Actually, this dysfunctional tribe of mine helped me build the coping skills I would need later when I would be out on my own at age sixteen. My self-protection instinct helped me to become a strong person. Yet, as I learned in the years ahead, the strong person I became fueled my need to do things my way, or as I called it, "the right way." My strengths gave way to blatant invulnerability, the Achilles Heel of self-protection—control.

Each of us has our own unique family story that plays a major role in shaping our perspectives and opinions. Some of you may have been raised as an only child or may have experienced a single-parent household. Others, like me, have experienced the chaos of a fluctuating family dynamic. These experiences bring their own influences which are amplified when there are additional wounds of neglect, betrayal, abuse, and loss. It can be natural for certain entitlements, deprivations, and distresses to encumber our worldviews. At the foundation of all family arrangements, self-efficacy can be at risk through the parenting or lack of parenting that we have received. The need to look out for "number one" or to self-protect at the expense of others, can emerge naturally in a world of potential threats. It is counterintuitive to follow the Golden Rule, to "do unto others as you would have them do unto you," if you see others as a potential threat to your welfare. So how do we outgrow the family maladjustments that can plague and destroy our future relationships? Once again, we need to return to our understanding of the source of our true identity.

This concept was illuminated a few years ago at a family lunch in Old Town, San Diego. After enjoying a feast of Mexican food and an afternoon strolling through the shops, our entire family walked together back to our cars. At this point, I (Mickey-also known as Boppa) lingered behind with my nine-year-old granddaughter, Kennedy. As Boppas tend to do, I lifted her up on my shoulders as we exchanged our thoughts on the best part of the day. Then came the fateful words that changed my life's perspective (and perhaps even my Last Will and Testament-all transferring to my Kennedy). My granddaughter looked down at my from her height above, leaned down and whispered into my ear, "Boppa, you're my favorite." Heartfelt, pure love expressed to another, without obligation or coercion, are some of the most gracious gifts that we can give to one another. And as you can imagine, my heart was about to burst as I whirled Kennedy down—to hug and kiss her cheek, while thanking her for making me feel so special.

After returning home, I was compelled to boast of Kennedy's loving whispers as I relayed the story to my wife and daughter, Julia, "Boppa you're my favorite!"

68

My wife, quickly asserted, "Oh yeah, earlier in the afternoon she said that to me as well." Then my daughter exclaimed, "What?! Kennedy said that to me when we were at lunch!" At that point the truth of pure love had saturated all of our hearts; whoever Kennedy was with at the moment, was her favorite. What a concept this has become for grasping a perspective of God's pure love for His sons and daughters! Whoever He is with, is His favorite. Emmanuel, "God with us." You are God's favorite! As we learn in Romans 8:14-17:

> " For as many as are led by the Spirit of God, these are sons of God. For you did not receive the spirit of bondage again to fear, but you received the Spirit of adoption by whom we cry out, 'Abba, Father.' The Spirit Himself bears witness with our spirit that we are children of God, and if children, then heirs—heirs of God and joint heirs with Christ, if indeed we suffer with Him, that we may also be glorified together" (NKJV).

Through a believing faith in Jesus Christ, the Scriptures declare that we become part of God's family (see John 1:12). We don't get religion, but instead, we get a deep relationship with the living God as our Father. We are adopted into His family as sons and daughters of the King of Kings, which means He is always with us. And as His favorite, He is always thinking of you! "How precious also are Your thoughts to me, O God! How great is the sum of them! If I should count them, they would be more in number than the sand; When I awake, I am still with You."[16]

God loves to speak to us and reveal Himself to us as His children. We are on God's mind all the time. "For I know the thoughts that I think toward you, says the LORD, thoughts of peace and not of evil, to give you a future and a hope. Then you will call upon Me and go and pray to Me, and I will listen to you. And you will seek Me and find Me when you search for Me with all your heart."[17] The Father heart of God is to spend time with us. He wants to guide us in our relationships and how we are to treat one another. God's plan from the beginning is for unity, love, and peace in our lives and families. Our early family situations are supposed to reflect our heavenly family perspective. Sadly, when this does not happen, self-assertion can become our survival mechanism.

As we look to the Word of God, we discover God's important truths that impact our daily living. Romans 12:1-2 speaks of this transformation:

"I beseech you therefore, brethren, by the
mercies of God, that you present your
bodies a living sacrifice, holy, acceptable
to God, which is your reasonable service.
And do not be conformed to this world,
but be transformed by the renewing of

---

[16] Psalm 139:17-18 (NKJV)

[17] Jeremiah 29:11-13 (NKJV). Context is of Judah, but God's heart behind this is for all of God's family.

your mind, that you may prove what is
that good and acceptable and perfect will
of God" (NKJV).

Knowing how much we are loved by God can transform
our perspectives on how we view all of our relationships.
God transforms us and empowers us to love others more
than self through the love we have experienced from
God.

Throughout the Scriptures we are encouraged to
make love preeminent: "Be kindly affectionate to one
another with brotherly love, in honor giving preference
to one another."[18] "Walk worthy of the calling with
which you were called, with all lowliness and gentleness,
with longsuffering, bearing with one another in love,
endeavoring to keep the unity of the Spirit in the bond of
peace."[19] "And be kind to one another, tenderhearted,
forgiving one another, even as God in Christ forgave
you."[20] "And you shall love the LORD your God with all
your heart, with all your soul, with all your mind, and
with all your strength.' This is the first commandment.
And the second, like this: 'You shall love your neighbor
as yourself.' There is no other commandment greater
than these."[21]

These truths lay a healthy foundation by which
we may serve others with love and humility. We can find

---

[18] Romans 12:10 (NKJV)

[19] Ephesians 4:1 (NKJV)

[20] Ephesians 4:32 (NKJV)

[21] Mark 12:30-31 (NKJV)

freedom from the old self-defending ways. Knowing that we are unconditionally loved by Jesus, we are assured that our painful past is wiped away and that we can now live freely in our new identity. We are His beloved children, treasured above all creation and made for relationship with our Father. It is from this secure place of value and love that we can move forward to love and serve each other. We can learn how to let go of the baggage of lies, wounds, and false identities that sabotage our relationships. We are enabled to operate in the truth, where we can love and be loved. We are restored to our original design as God intended from the beginning. The truth is, we are all unique individuals, one of a kind. We are loved, chosen, made in God's image, and highly valued by our Father. Our identity is not based on our family, job, income, education, or anything of this world. Our identity is based on His assessment of our worth. It is possible that even the most horrific aspects of our past can be healed over time. However, we recognize that for some, this may need more intensive assistance from a qualified counselor or support system.

A favorite book of ours by Andrew Murray is a classic for growing in this

challenge. As previously mentioned, the book is appropriately entitled, Humility. Ponder these thoughts as you grow in your freedom from self:

> "The humble man seeks at all times to act
> according to the Scriptures: 'with honor
> preferring one another; by love serve one

another; esteeming others better than themselves; submitting yourselves one to another.' The question is often asked, 'how can we count others better than ourselves, when we see that they are far below us in wisdom, holiness, natural gifts, or grace received?' The question itself proves at once how little we understand what real lowliness of mind is. True humility comes when, in the light of God, we have seen ourselves to be nothing and have consented to part with and cast away self, to let God's Spirit rule in us. The person that has done this, and can say, 'I have lost myself in finding Him,' no longer compares itself with others. It has given up forever every thought of self in God's presence. It interacts with its fellow man as one who is nothing and seeks nothing for itself. This person is a servant of God, and for His sake, a servant of all. A faithful servant may be wiser than the master and still retain the true spirit and attitude of the servant. Let us look at every person who annoys or irritates us, as God's means of grace, God's instrument for our purification, for the working out of humility. Jesus, our life, breathes within us. And let us have such faith in the completeness of God, and the nothingness of self, that as nothing in our own eyes, we may, in God's power, only seek to serve one another in love."[22]

Or, as C.S. Lewis so aptly affirmed, "Humility is not thinking less of yourself, it's thinking of yourself less."

---

[22] Murray, Andrew. (1982). *Humility*. New Kensington, PA: Whitaker House.

Reflect-Respond-Renew

1) Identifying behaviors and motives. Reflect on the following questions. As you ponder these questions, seek to have an honest awareness of your feelings and attitudes:

- How often do I care for the needs of others before my own?
- Do I seek to build up others when I have the opportunity?
- Do others see me as a selfish or generous person in how I handle my time, money, or talents?
- At times, am I manipulative or self-seeking in getting my needs met?
- Am I a people-pleaser seeking not to be rejected by others?
- Am I ok sharing my honest feelings with others?
- Do I feel safe, accepted, and loved in my close relationships?

2) Believe the Biblical truths of what God affirms of His children in the Bible:

- I have been given all things that pertain to life and godliness. (2 Peter 1:3)
- I am filled with all the fullness of God. (Ephesians 3:19)

- I am empowered to walk in the Spirit. (Galatians 5:22-25)
- I am able to be kindly affectionate to others with brotherly love, in honor. (Romans 12:10)

3) Action Steps:

- Identify someone that you can personally affirm and build up this week. Plan out specifically what you are going to say to encourage them.
- Lay down your preference and let another have their way in a decision.
- Memorize one of the promises above that speaks of your identity and say it out loud throughout the day.
- Seek to be a more attentive listener today with the goal to understand another's point of view.
- Say a prayer over any current challenges and give them to God. Let go.

Chapter Eight
Father Knows Best

The wisdom of the ages affirms that those who do not learn from history are doomed to repeat it. Building on this concept, it has been stated that experience is the most brutal of teachers. But you learn. My God, do you learn! Experience and history are definitely wise instructors, if we open ourselves to learn the lessons we must, and avoid repeating the same mistakes. My (Karen's) personal history is proof enough that this concept is right. My journey is a testimony of discovering God's rule in human affairs. When we surrender to His gracious interruptions, blessings can ensue. And for the benefit of future generations, it is crucial to know that one's history can be salvaged for a transformed future.

There was a family TV show in the 1960's we used to watch as kids called Father Knows Best. The fictitious dad was a young good-looking guy who was without fault. He always said and did everything just perfectly. However, when we think about God as our heavenly Father, He is in reality, "perfect in all of His ways." We have learned that life's choices can be better when guided by our Father's eternal vantage point and wisdom.

We all have choices to make throughout our lifetime; some major, others rather insignificant to the course of our lives. Most of us think that we know what is best for ourselves, but often the decisions we make aren't the wisest ones. Basically, we want to be in control of our destiny even though we are very limited in our perspectives. Oftentimes we are influenced negatively by our traumatic experiences or unhealthy desires which shape the way that we think and act. This was certainly true about me. And I approached my twenties with great excitement. I had been out on my own since my junior year of high school.

Somehow, I ended up living in the San Francisco Bay area. My friends were wealthy and much older than me and knew how to have a good time. Going to Las Vegas, Lake Tahoe, horse races, riding in limousines, meeting celebrities, and elegant dining at some of the finest restaurants were the realities of my life back then. As you might guess, I eventually ended up engaged to one of the older wealthy gentlemen. Life was a lot of fun as I got to drive fancy sports cars, sit in front row seats at Lakers games and do pretty much whatever we wanted. Then one beautiful summer day, everything changed.

It was an unforgettable day, the day when I stumbled upon a book that changed the direction of my life. On one of my many days of leisure, I decided to layout by the pool and read a book. I went to the bookshelf to find an entertaining read, when a leather-bound book caught my eye. I pulled it off of the shelf and realized that it was the Bible my older brother had sent me in the previous year. "Huh," I thought, "I've never read the Bible before." Having had a Catholic upbringing, I was vaguely familiar with its content, but curiosity and providence led me to read it for the very first time on that particular day. I opened it to the Gospel of John in the New Testament and started reading, "In the beginning was the Word, and the Word was with God and the Word was God... And the Word became flesh and dwelt among us.... full of grace and truth."[23] These words pierced my heart like a sharp arrow. For the first time in my life, I began to understand that the distant God I believed in was actually near and knowable. I had wondered for many years why God had created this world, and then just left us on our own to figure it all out. The country was going through some very tumultuous times. The Vietnam War was ending, drugs were pervasive and promiscuity was widely accepted. Where was God in all of this confusion?

The many years of going to Mass and Catholic school had failed to teach me that God wanted to be a Father to me; a Friend, Teacher, and so much more. Wow, I realized, He cared about ME! The choices and details of my life were of great interest to Him. I was His daughter and He was my Father. I began to read the Bible every day, and I started learning who God is, and what His plans and purposes were for my life. Verses like Hebrews 11:6 became truths by which my life would be guided, "But without faith, it is impossible to please Him, for he who comes to God must believe that He is and that He is a rewarder of those who diligently seek Him" (NKJV). Jeremiah 31:3 also revealed to me, "I have loved you with an everlasting love; Therefore with

---

[23] John 1:1, 14 (NKJV)

lovingkindness I have drawn you" (NKJV). My faith began to grow and I realized that God's plans were bigger and better than my own as He only loved me.

Life was about to take on a whole new direction for me with this decision to follow God's path rather than my own. I started to trust that God, being all-wise, all-knowing and perfect in all of His ways, knew what was best for me. At this point in my life, I was now engaged to and living with a much older wealthy Jewish man. To make matters even more challenging, I was also working for him. My new-found faith, however, encouraged me not to marry outside of my Christian faith. So, I had a choice to make: continue in the comfortable lifestyle I had grown so accustomed to, or honor God's plan for my life, trusting that He knew better.

As I considered my options, a litany of questions arose. Where would I live? How would I take care of myself? What should I do next? I could settle in where I was, or take a leap of faith towards what I knew in my heart was right. I could follow the course God had chartered for me, or do life my way. As I weighed my decision, Hebrews 11:6 kept echoing in my heart: "He is a rewarder of those who diligently seek Him" (NKJV).

As a faithful Father, God doesn't leave us on our own to figure it all out. He comes to us with all of His gentleness and applies the healing balm of His love to the fearful and hurting places in our hearts. He gives us His Word like a light for our paths and guides us in the way of peace. But in order for us to experience all that

He promises us, we have to give over control of our lives to Him. The importance of surrender and the ability to move into greater faith is based on knowing and obeying God. I was growing in my relationship with my heavenly Father, and the byproduct of this was now changing the way I lived. When we are able to trust the omnipotent (all-power) and omniscient (all-knowing) God, we are led to the sacred place of surrender and enabled to let go. His Spirit and His Word become our compass.

Fast-forward forty years later. The decision I made to follow Jesus that day by the pool was the most life-changing choice in my sixty-years of living. As a result of my obedience to God, I met my amazing husband at the church I started attending. Mickey is the love of my life and he has shown, taught, and modeled for me more about God and living a life of faith than anyone else. The journey we have been on has been full of adventure, travel, fun, laughter, and most of all, love. Who knew? God did! I thought I was giving up so much to yield to God when in reality, I gained so much more than I could have ever imagined.

The other day while I was perusing social media, a post by a good friend, Courtney, stopped me in my tracks. There it was, the perfect synopsis of the struggle of surrender. She wrote:

> "I like to be in control. To know the plan. To be prepared. To have all the facts. In life, I get overwhelmed when there are too many options with no clear decision or path. I try to control the

uncontrollable. I play out every scenario
in my head to the point of exhaustion.
God has been reminding me that I've
never been in control. He has been in
control. He knows the plans ... the best
ones by the way. So, I relinquish my
thoughts and plans to Him. And what do
I find—Freedom. Freedom to let go and
trust Him. Freedom to not have to have
every answer. Freedom to live by faith.
Freedom from fear. Freedom to obey.
FREEDOM. Wow. Let's all shout that
out loud together shall we? 1, 2, 3:
FREEDOM! Phew, feels good doesn't
it?"

We couldn't have said this any better. Our Father truly
knows best. And who knows, maybe as you are reading
this very chapter, there's an important choice to be
made soon in your life. If so, pause, go to your bookshelf,
grab that Bible and start asking God to reveal His love
and wisdom to you.

Reflect-Respond-Renew

1) Identifying behaviors and motives. Reflect on the following questions. As you ponder these questions, seek to have an honest awareness of your feelings and attitudes:

- Are there areas in my life where I don't completely trust God? Why do you think that is?
- Do I trust and believe that God loves me and my family and that He only has our best interests in mind?
- Is there an area of my life where I know I'm being disobedient to my heavenly Father?

2) Believe the Biblical truths of what God affirms of His children in the Bible:

- "Daniel answered and said: 'Blessed be the name of God forever and ever, for wisdom and might are His.'" (Daniel 2:20 NKJV).
- "Oh, the depth of the riches both of the wisdom and knowledge of God! How unsearchable are His judgments and His ways past finding out?" (Romans 11:33 NKJV).
- "Trust in the LORD with all your heart, and lean not on your own

understanding; in all your ways acknowledge Him, and He shall direct your paths. Do not be wise in your own eyes; fear the LORD and depart from evil" (Proverbs 3:4-7 NKJV).

- "To obey is better than sacrifice" (1 Samuel 15:22 NKJV).
- "For those who honor Me, I will honor" (1 Samuel 2:30 NKJV).

3) Action Steps:

- Ask God for His help and wisdom when you make your next decision.
- Memorize one of the promises of God above and say it out loud throughout the day.
- Look for one situation where you shouldn't lean on your limited perspective and stop, pray, and ask God for His help and guidance.
- Write a letter to your Father God telling Him how much you want to trust Him and how you want to let Him lead your life. Start making daily declarations that God has the lead over these areas. God knows how you feel and He will lead you in every step of faith you take.

Chapter Nine
Getting Over-Parenting

Parenting is a wonderful adventure that comes without instruction manuals. Most of us figure things out through trial and error, no matter how much research we've done. To be sure, as parents, we have made many mistakes along the way, but by the grace of God, our kids have grown up to be amazing adults. Still, we have continued to be tutored in our aging roles as empty nesters and as grandparents. It is incredible that the temptation to be in control does not diminish over the lifecycle; it's just more subtle in its maneuvering.

When our oldest daughter and her husband wanted to buy their first home, we were able to assist them with a loan for their down payment. One afternoon I (Karen) was over at my daughter's new place and she was telling me about a few upgrades that they were planning to make. Without thinking I blurted out, "You can't afford that!" She quickly retorted, "This isn't any of your concern." After a brief internal struggle, I realized that she was absolutely right! It was not my place to tell her and her husband how to spend their money. I quickly responded with, "You are so right, I'm sorry." You see, I believed that I had a say-so because we had lent them money. I needed to make sure that they were not careless or extravagant with our money, so as to be sure that we would be paid back. But I suddenly realized that my motive was grounded in my need to control how another grown adult prioritized her budget.

I had stepped over boundaries where I had not been invited. There's a very natural desire the stems from love, for parents to over-parent at all stages of their children's lives. Providing sound counsel when requested is welcome, but very different from asserting one's uninvited opinions.

Throughout our years together as mentors, we've often heard parents confessing their manipulation, guilting, coercion, and bribery of their grown children, into doing or not doing something they wanted. We have heard far too many testimonies of broken families and stonewalled relationships, where parents have failed to acknowledge or give up their control tactics. Sadly, there can be a fine line between empowering and being in power, as it relates to our child-rearing practices. Great wisdom is gained in Bob and Judy Hughes' book, Love Focused, where they instruct:

> "Our effort to control people and things is by far the most damaging strategy we use in our attempt to achieve Outcome Focused Goals. Because our success depends on other people doing what we need them to do, we end up using people for our own purposes and not truly loving them. Some of the greatest damage done to love occurs as the result of our attempts to control the outcomes in our lives, because love is always sacrificed to control."[24]

People are never to be used or seen as a means to an end. In God's economy, people are the priority in His plan. Once again, to love God and to love people are the ultimate fulfillment of God's challenge to humanity. The need to control and to exercise power over others is an affront to love. The nature of love is to empower and to build others up, rather than to have power over them. Such was the lesson Jesus had to teach His followers:

> "But Jesus called them to Himself and said to them, 'You know that those who are considered rulers over the Gentiles lord it over them and their great ones exercise authority over them. Yet it shall not be so among you; but whoever desires to become great among you shall be your servant. And whoever of you desires to be first shall be servant of all. For even the Son of Man did not come to be served, but to serve and to give His life a ransom for many.'"[25]

If we live to empower others in love, we should naturally want God's greatest good in their lives. This doesn't involve manipulation or coercion but instead, sacrificial service. What a concept Jesus left the world when He declared, "Greater love has no one than this,

[24] Hughes, Bob and Judy. (2008). *Love Focused,* New York, New York: Crossroads.
[25] Matthew 20:25 (NKJV).

than to lay down one's life for his friends."[26] The next time you are urged to control your grown kids' situation, pause and ask yourself, "How can I best love and serve them?"

Though this perspective is honorable, letting go is hard; especially if we're used to controlling others. But perhaps a lesson from the Kerala monkeys in India will provide some encouragement to you. Banana plantations are profitable in Kerala. However, local monkeys can take a toll on profits. In the early years, farmers tried everything to stop the monkeys from eating the plantation's bananas, with little success. The monkeys outsmarted every security attempt—from guard dogs to fences, to various traps with loud noises. It wasn't until the farmers discovered a fatal weakness in the monkey's temperament that success was finally achieved. The farmers bored a small hole in one of the ends of a raw coconut and stuffed it with sweetmeats and rice. They then tethered the other end to a stake and placed it in a clearing. When a monkey smelled the treats inside, it would reach into the coconut to grasp the snack.

The challenge for the monkey was that the hole was just small enough for its hand to reach in and grab the tasty treasure. However, once the hand was clasped around the treat it couldn't be pulled back out of the small hole. After the monkey put its hand into the coconut, the Keralite farmers would simply walk up to

---

[26] John 15:13 (NKJV)

the monkey and capture it. As the Keralites approached, the primate would screech in frustration as it couldn't get the food out of the coconut with a clenched fist. If the monkeys simply let go, their hands could easily slip back out of the coconut and they would be free. Yet, with clenched fists, their fates were determined.

Which begs the question; what are you clinging to in relation to circumstances, people, past wounds, addictions, failures or successes that have you trapped? Perhaps it's time to relax your grip. The promise of freedom awaits you if you'll just open your heart and let go.

Reflect-Respond-Renew

1) Identifying behaviors and motives. Reflect on the following questions. As you ponder these challenges, seek to have an honest awareness of your feelings and attitudes:

- In what is an area that you feel the most out of control?
- What are you afraid will happen if you let go of control and trust others?
- Do you believe that God loves you and only has your best interests in mind?
- Do you really believe you have control over your family and the outcomes of their lives?
- Is there a past situation that has caused you not to trust God for your family? Why?

2) Believe the Biblical truths of what God affirms of His children in the Bible:

- "For GOD is sheer beauty, all-generous in love, loyal always and ever" (Psalm 100:5 The Message Bible).
- "For with You is the fountain of life; in Your light, we see light" (Psalm 36:9 NKJV).

- "Christ the power of God and the wisdom of God" (1 Corinthians 1:24 NKJV).
- "A man's heart plans his way, but the Lord directs his steps" (Proverbs 16:9 NKJV).
- "For in Him all things were created: things in heaven and on earth, visible and invisible, whether thrones or powers or rulers or authorities; all things have been created through Him and for Him" (Colossians 1:16 NIV).

3) Action Steps:

- Sincerely pray, and ask God to help you trust Him more from the depths of your heart.
- Memorize one of the promises of God above and say it out loud all day.
- Look for one situation where you can stop, pray, and listen for God's leading in a matter or decision.
- Be mindful of your attitude, tone of voice, or comments where there might be prideful motives in your family relationships.
- Pray for God to prompt your heart to let go.

- Find someone who will walk this journey of freedom with you and establish an accountability relationship.

Chapter Ten
Out of Control-Leadership

By now you may be thinking, "OK, I get it. I need to let go of trying to manipulate others for my own personal benefit. So, does this mean that I just become a compliant follower with no will of my own?" The answer, of course, is "no!" Being out of control does not necessarily mean that you surrender all aspects of your will and influence. Influence, when properly leveraged, is at the core of being a good leader. However, the heart of the matter is a matter of the heart. In this chapter, we will explore the nature of leadership as it relates to power, influence, and interpersonal transformation.

One of the greatest gifts in life is becoming grandparents. You get to relive many of the joys you had with your own children, but when the grandkids get cranky, sick or troublesome, you just give them back to their parents. You get to recreate so many of the fun family memories without having to deal with any of the downsides. Fortunately for us, all of our grandchildren are amazing.

When our oldest granddaughter was just a preschooler, we often had the pleasure of babysitting her and her younger brother. On one such occasion, we took the kids to a nearby park with their plastic beach toys. As our precious grandchildren began to make castles with their buckets and shovels, another youngster moved into their space and started using their playthings. Naturally, our little ones were annoyed, so they picked up their toys and moved a few yards away. Within minutes, the new acquaintance followed closely behind and settled back in to play with their sand toys. I realized that this was a teachable moment to learn about sharing. I told my sweet grandkids, "Sometimes it's nice to share with a new friend." My granddaughter promptly responded, "Sometimes it's nice to share, and sometimes it's OK not to share. This is one of those times." With that, she whisked her toys away and relocated herself a third time. In that instant, I realized that I was being schooled by a five-year-old on the art of leadership through the wisdom of cuteness.

The dynamics of influence and control start at a very early age. Most of us are prone to manage our relationships with self-assertion and self-protection as core motives. As we discussed previously, because of past wounds and stresses, our natural trigger is to protect ourselves from experiencing further pain. At a subconscious level, whenever we experience a potential threat, the midbrain is wired to resist (fight) or escape (flight). When a real danger exists, this is a good thing. However, this sometimes translates into an emotional outburst of anger, anxiety or relational withdrawal as a reaction to a perceived threat that may not actually exist. Over time, these experiences can grow in intensity and be displayed through rage, phobias, depression, and a whole host of other maladies.

Years ago, at a workshop, I (Mickey) became acquainted with a brain specialist from the Veterans Administration Hospital in San Diego. He worked exclusively with Traumatic Brain Injury (TBI) and Post-Traumatic Stress Injury clients. In my life's experience, I had noticed that people who had TBI seemed to struggle with rage. I asked this therapist about how many of his clients struggled with bouts of anger, and he responded that it was close to 100%. Because of previous trauma, the logical override system of the brain can be bypassed. As such, the midbrain sparks the fight/flight response into action when it senses a similar experience associated with a previous threat. Anger (fight) and isolation (flight) are common reactions of people who have been injured in the past, when there is a subconscious perceived threat.

The specialist went on to provide a very dynamic example that helped me more fully grasp this significance. Over the years, the VA Hospital had noticed that in the month of August in San Diego, there tended to be a spike in the number of Vietnam veterans who struggled with Post Traumatic Stress Disorder symptoms. The doctor explained that in August, San Diego has higher humidity, which is similar to the monsoonal weather patterns in Vietnam. The muggy weather with tropical plant smells and cumulonimbus cloud formations trigger the veteran's brains to fire off alarms which result in nightmares, anxiety, depression, agitation and/or anger. These are normal reactions in normal people, but in these instances are triggered by a past traumatic experience.

Now you may not be a veteran with combat experience, but all of us have had painful events that are stored in our memory banks. God has hardwired us with a need for love, safety, security, and other natural healthy fundamentals. When these needs feel threatened, our brains fire off in self-protection mode. This is where self-awareness is essential. Rather than being a victim to our default coping mechanisms, God empowers us to break past cycles of reactions, so that we can experience the freedom that comes through our faith in Him. When we understand who we are in our identity and in Whose we are in love; trust, safety, and security can grow. This is how our relationship with God transforms our reactions to the threats in our daily circumstances. And yes, discipleship, counseling, mentors, life-coaches, and other life investments will benefit this growth. There are many triggers that govern our motives and interactions in our relationships. Whatever they are, we need to identify them, and how they impact our desire for control.

At our core, we either seek to control others for our personal benefit, or we seek the virtue of mutuality that seeks the welfare of all. There's a very subtle difference in one's intentions to need to have power over others or to desire to empower others. Unhealthy people tend to take control of their surroundings and become dominant and dysfunctional leaders that are inclined to rule over others for their own personal gain. Virtuous leadership, on the other hand, empowers people to become the best versions of who they are meant to be.

Whatever masters our core motives and actions, dictates the substance and legacy of our lives. If God is our Master, He will free us to reach our fullest potential, by empowering us to reflect the Person of Jesus Christ in character, actions, motives, words, and attitudes. As the ancient Chinese proverb goes, "If planning for a year, grow rice. If planning for a decade, grow trees. If planning for centuries, grow people." Perhaps you've heard the old adage, "hurting people, hurt people." Isn't it just as true to say that "loved people, love people," and "encouraged people, encourage people?" Your healing will lead to the healing of others, just as the love you receive from God will help you love them the way He designed you to.

There was once an aged man who revealed that when he was young, he wanted to change the world. When he grew older, he perceived that this was too ambitious, so he set out to change his state. This too, he realized as he grew older was too ambitious, so he set out to change his town. When he realized he couldn't even do this, he tried to change his family. Now as an old man, he decided that he should have started by changing himself. If he had started with himself, maybe then he would have succeeded in changing his family, the town, or even the state — and who knows, maybe even the world!

Reflect-Respond-Renew

1) Identifying behaviors and motives. Reflect on the following questions. As you ponder these questions, seek to have an honest awareness of your feelings, motives, and attitudes.

- Are you free to admit to others your own weaknesses and failures?
- Are you open to pursuing a mentor, counselor, or coach for your own personal growth?
- Are you approachable and open to input and / or correction from others?
- How do you build a sense of trust with those you are leading?
- Are you vulnerable about your own shortcomings and gracious with the faults of others?
- Do you see people as a resource to accomplish your goals or as gifts to be loved and empowered?
- Do you tend to project blame on others or to seek ways to grow others when there are challenges?

2) Believe the Biblical truths of what God affirms His heart for leadership:

- "And He Himself gave some to be apostles, some prophets, some evangelists, and some pastors and teachers, for the equipping of the saints for the work of ministry, for the edifying of the body of Christ, till we all come to the unity of the faith and of the knowledge of the Son of God, to a perfect man, to the measure of the stature of the fullness of Christ" (Ephesians 4:11-13 NKJV).
- "But Jesus called them to Himself and said, 'You know that the rulers of the Gentiles lord it over them, and those who are great exercise authority over them. Yet it shall not be so among you; but whoever desires to become great among you, let him be your servant. And whoever desires to be first among you, let him be your slave—just as the Son of Man did not come to be served, but to serve, and to give His life a ransom for many'" (Matthew 20:25-28 NKJV).
- "Him we preach, warning every man and teaching every man in all wisdom, that we may present every man perfect in Christ Jesus" (Colossians 1:28 NKJV).

- "But Jesus called them to Himself and said to them, 'You know that those who are considered rulers over the Gentiles lord it over them, and their great ones exercise authority over them. Yet it shall not be so among you; but whoever desires to become great among you shall be your servant. And whoever of you desires to be first shall be slave of all. For even the Son of Man did not come to be served, but to serve, and to give His life a ransom for many'" (Mark 10:42-44 NKJV).

3) Action Steps:

In your journal, write out a list of the people and relationships you are involved in where you have influence. What is one thing that you can do to purposely empower another person to grow in their potential? For example, identify a virtue that you see in a co-worker or friend that would benefit from encouragement. Intentionally encourage this person through words of affirmation, a letter, text, email, or some other form of communication.

Chapter Eleven
Conclusion of the Whole Matter

While journaling this morning, I happened to reflect on a book that I (Mickey) wrote a few years ago called, GODISNOWHERE. There's an intentional interplay in how one might read this title; either "God Is Now Here" or, "God Is Nowhere." Without much thought, I scribbled down in my journal the phrase GODISINCONTROL. To my surprise, the same interplay can be found as well. Either "God Is In Control" or, "God I Sin Control." Perhaps that's a stretch, but I had to chuckle over the fact that there are basically only two ways to live out our lives; with Him in charge or us, in sin, trying to control our own lives and others.

King Solomon considered all of his life's incredible accomplishments, triumphs, mistakes, and failings, and determined that a relationship with God was the key to humanity's wellbeing and contentment. Such was his final thoughts, expressed in the book of Ecclesiastes, "Let us hear the conclusion of the whole matter: Fear God and keep His commandments, for this is man's all."[27] As the wisest, richest, and most powerful man who ever lived, King Solomon learned that submitting to God in reverence and honor was that most important and fulfilling thing we could ever do for ourselves.

---

[27] Ecclesiastes 12:13 (NKJV)

We would be wise to end the thoughts in this book with his conclusion as well. There is no greater place of peace and freedom than to daily abide in a position of close proximity to our heavenly Father. Only then can we know with complete confidence, God's great love, power, mercy, and authority over all things. This is where we find the freedom from our wounds and past traumas, and ultimately, our need to control.

Our individual journeys of freedom began by the two of us each separately starting to read the Bible. Before Karen and I, Mickey, ever met I started reading the Bible in the Gospel of Matthew, and Karen in the Gospel of John. A few years later, we met and start reading the Bible together. We discovered that God has a great plan for each of us individually, and as a couple, and that the sooner we get on board with His plan, the sooner we would be empowered to soar.

Early in our marriage, Karen was looking through some old photos and came across a number of pictures of her baptism in Mission Bay, San Diego. As a new Christian, Karen was fully committed to her pursuit of God, which led her to make a public declaration of her faith in getting baptized. This event took place a year before we met. But as we looked through those pictures together, we realized that her future husband (I) was in all of them. I was in the bay at the same time, baptizing another person just a few feet away from Karen. There were a couple of pictures that actually captured us walking past each other heading in and out of the water. We couldn't help but to laugh at the providence of God. He knew His plans for us before we ever even met, and in light of those pictures, we are pretty sure there was a giggle in heaven as God would one day bring us together as husband and wife. Truly, GODISINCONTROL!

So, how do we move into this place of freedom each day, with the weight of so much hurt in our lives? It's critical that we take the time to look hard and long at our motives and inclinations for exerting control over others. In prayer, God will reveal the broken parts of our hearts, and help us heal. Our job is to go to Him for healing.

Through many twists and turns in life, we have learned that sorrow and guilt tend to look back, worry looks ahead, doubt looks around, but faith looks up! It is very easy to fall prey to our circumstances when we are prone to struggle with anxiety, depression, or anger. The tendency to be distressed or frustrated about the annoyances, pressures, and injustices that come upon us is a very human and normal response. But God promises us freedom from these natural responses when we adjust to His perspectives. In fact, Scriptures encourage alternative reactions to our challenges, that are usually the opposite of how we would naturally react. That's because, in looking up, we see things not from our perspectives, but from God's. This alters how we respond, by overriding our natural instincts with faith and trust in God's providence and provision. In the Bible, we learn that King David experienced an overwhelming degree of offenses and difficulties. Yet, God led him to a peaceful place of wisdom:

> "Do not fret because of evildoers, nor be envious of the workers of iniquity… Trust in the LORD, and do good; dwell in the land, and feed on His faithfulness. Delight yourself also in the LORD, and He shall give you the desires of your heart. Commit your way to the LORD, trust also in Him, and He shall bring it to pass. He shall bring forth your righteousness as the light, and your justice as the noonday. Rest in the LORD, and wait patiently for Him; do not fret because of him who prospers in his way, because of the man who brings wicked schemes to pass. Cease from anger, and forsake wrath; do not fret—it only causes harm."[28]

Fretting, anger, and wrath can truly harm our psyche, even though they're normal responses to injustice and stress. The Lord's antithetical encouragements seem almost humorous, in light of how we sometimes feel. But God urges us to respond the way He tells us to by trusting, delighting, resting, and ceasing—no matter how we feel. This is where faith becomes our source of hope

---

[28] Psalm 37:1-8 (NKJV).

in the midst of hurt; peace in the midst of pain; and freedom in the midst of failure.

As you start trusting God, you will take on new perspectives about yourself, others and about life altogether. Your freedom will grow day-by-day, moment-by-moment, and decision-by-decision as you surrender each step to God's control. He's transformed our lives, and the lives of countless others, and we invite you to join us in this lifelong journey. Freedom is yours if only you let go. So together, let's get out of control, and trust that **GOD IS IN CONTROL!**

Made in the USA
San Bernardino, CA
06 June 2020

72759154R00060